# INSPIRING LIVES

# KATHLEEN BATTLE
## American Soprano

By Livia Franke

**Gareth Stevens**
Publishing

Please visit our Web site www.garethstevens.com. For a free color catalog of all our high-quality books, call toll free 1-800-542-2595 or fax 1-877-542-2596.

Library of Congress Cataloging-in-Publication Data

Franke, Livia.
 Kathleen Battle : American soprano / Livia Franke.
    p. cm. — (Inspiring lives)
 Includes index.
 ISBN 978-1-4339-3635-7 (pbk.)
 ISBN 978-1-4339-3636-4 (6-pack)
 ISBN 978-1-4339-3634-0 (library binding)
 1. Battle, Kathleen—Juvenile literature. 2. Sopranos (Singers)—United States—Biography—Juvenile literature. I. Title.
 ML3930.B34F73 2010
 782.1092—dc22
 [B]
                               2009037273

Published in 2010 by Gareth Stevens Publishing
111 East 14th Street, Suite 349
New York, NY 10003

Copyright © 2010 Gareth Stevens Publishing

Designer: Daniel Hosek
Editor: Therese Shea

Photo credits: Cover (Battle), title page (Battle) © Kevin Parry/WireImage/Getty Images; cover (orchestra) © Awad Awad/AFP/Getty Images; cover (opera house), title page (opera house) © Martin Buerau/AFP/Getty Images; pp. 5, 15, 19 © Beatriz Schiller/Time & Life Pictures/Getty Images; pp. 7, 11, 17, 23 © Johan Elbers/Time & Life Pictures/Getty Images; p. 9 © Kevin Kane/WireImage/Getty Images; p. 13 © Scott Wintrow/Getty Images; p. 21 © Ron Scherl/Redferns/Getty Images; p. 25 © Frank Micelotta/Getty Images; p. 27 © Spencer Platt/Getty Images; p. 29 © Brian Ach/WireImage/Getty Images.

Printed in the United States of America

CPSIA compliance information: Batch #CW10GS: For further information contact Gareth Stevens, New York, New York at 1-800-542-2595.

# Contents

# A Beautiful Voice

Kathleen Battle is an opera singer. She is a soprano.

# Growing Up Singing

Kathleen was born in Portsmouth, Ohio, in 1948. She was the youngest of seven children.

OHIO

Columbus

Portsmouth

Kathleen sang at church. She had a beautiful voice.

# Music School

Kathleen studied music in school. A teacher told her to never stop singing.

Kathleen wanted to be a music teacher.

She began teaching music in 1971.

# Kathleen's Big Break

In 1972, a conductor heard Kathleen sing.

He asked her to sing in Italy.

Kathleen sang in her first opera in 1975. The next year, she sang in an opera in New York City.

# A Rising Star

Kathleen worked hard. She learned about each opera. She studied the music.

Operas tell a story. Kathleen made sure her singing helped tell the story.

Kathleen became a star! She sang in opera houses all over the world.

# All Kinds of Music

Today, Kathleen sings all different kinds of music. She sings with other famous singers, too.

Queen Latifah

Alicia Keys

Kathleen sings at concerts. She sang for the U.S. president in 1992.

# Still Singing

Kathleen has won many music awards.

She will keep singing for years to come!

# Timeline

**1948**  Kathleen is born in Portsmouth, Ohio.

**1971**  Kathleen becomes a music teacher.

**1972**  A conductor hears Kathleen sing.

**1975**  Kathleen sings in her first opera.

**1976**  Kathleen sings in New York City.

**1985**  Kathleen wins her first major award.

**1992**  Kathleen sings for the president of the United States.

# For More Information

## Books:

Hines, Jerome. *Great Singers on Great Singing: A Famous Opera Star Interviews 40 Famous Opera Singers on the Technique of Singing.* New York: Limelight Editions, 2004.

Shahrukh, Husain. *Stories from the Opera.* Cambridge, MA: Barefoot Books, 2007.

## Web Sites:

Columbia Artists Management Inc.: Vocal: Soprano: Kathleen Battle
**www.cami.com/?webid=27**

Kathleen Battle (Soprano)
**www.bach-cantatas.com/Bio/Battle-Kathleen.htm**

# Glossary

**award:** a prize given to someone for doing something well

**concert:** a public music event

**conductor:** one who leads musicians and singers as they play and sing

**opera:** a play that is sung to music

**soprano:** a person who can sing the highest parts in an opera

# Index